DANGEROUS MAMMALS

MOUNTAIN LIONS

Kim Thompson

NorwoodHouse Press

Cataloging-in-Publication Data

Names: Thompson, Kim, 1970-.
Title: Mountain lions / Kim Thompson.
Description: Buffalo, NY : Norwood House Press, 2026. | Series: Dangerous mammals | Includes glossary and index.
Identifiers: ISBN 9781978577435 (pbk.) | ISBN 9781978577442 (library bound) | ISBN 9781978577459 (ebook)
Subjects: LCSH: Puma--Juvenile literature.
Classification: LCC QL737.C23 T474 2026 | DDC 599.7524--dc23

Published in 2026 by
Norwood House Press
2544 Clinton Street
Buffalo, NY 14224

Designer: Rhea Magaro

Photo credits: Cover, pp. 1, 10, 12 Evgeniyqw/Shutterstock.com; p. 5 Jim Cumming/Shutterstock.com; p. 6 JoeFotos/Shutterstock.com; p. 7 Bill Perry/Shutterstock.com; p. 8 Georgia Evans/Shutterstock.com; p. 11 Christina Moraes/Shutterstock.com; p. 13 Dennis W Donohue/Shutterstock.com; p. 15 Dennis MacDonald/Shutterstock.com; p. 16 Kathryn Bakken/Shutterstock.com; p. 17 taviphoto/Shutterstock.com; p. 18 lalcreative/Shutterstock.com; p. 19 Diego Grandi/Shutterstock.com; p. 21 Debbie Steinhausser/Shutterstock.com

Printed in the United States of America

CPSIA compliance information: Batch #CWNHP26: For further information contact Norwood House Press at 1-800-237-9932.

TABLE OF CONTENTS

MEET THE MOUNTAIN LION

A mountain lion is a big cat. Its huge **range** covers much of North America and South America.

In different areas, these **mammals** are called by different names. They are known as cougars, panthers, and pumas.

Their fur comes in many colors. Their chests are often white.

A mountain lion is about the same size as an adult person. Mountain lions can grow to be over five feet (one and one-half meters) long. They can weigh over 100 pounds (45 kilograms).

Mountain lions have sharp **vision** and excellent hearing. Their sense of smell is poor, though.

Their back legs are powerful. These cats can leap the length of a city bus! They can jump straight up in the air more than 18 feet (five meters)!

Mountain lions have **adapted** to many environments. They live wherever there is **prey**.

They can be found in mountains, forests, deserts, and swamps. Some live near people in towns and cities.

FAVORITE FOODS

Mountain lions are excellent hunters. These **carnivores** eat small animals like birds, rabbits, and raccoons. They eat larger animals like deer and elk. Some attack farm animals such as cows and sheep.

Mountain lions **stalk** their prey. They wait for the right moment to **pounce**. Then, they bite the animal's neck.

After a hunt, they will hide some of the meat for a later meal.

STAYING SAFE AROUND MOUNTAIN LIONS

Mountain lions keep to themselves. They rarely attack humans.

If you know mountain lions are nearby, be alert. Keep pets close to you. Do not walk alone in the early morning and evening when the cats are most active.

If you see a mountain lion, stop. Do not run. Look in the cat's eyes.

Yell, wave your arms, and throw things. If you give the animal some space, it will usually move on.

GLOSSARY

adapted (uh-DAP-tid): changed over time to fit better in a place or situation

carnivores (KAHR-nuh-vorz): animals that eat meat

mammals (MAM-uhlz): animals that are warm-blooded, have hair or fur, and feed milk to their babies

pounce (pouns): to jump forward and grab something suddenly

prey (pray): animals that are hunted and eaten by other animals

range (raynj): the area where an animal naturally lives and travels

stalk (stawk): to follow or track an animal quietly and carefully before attacking

vision (VIZH-uhn): the sense of sight; the ability to see

THINKING QUESTIONS

1. On what continents do mountain lions live?
2. What are some other names for mountain lions?
3. How does a mountain lion's body help it hunt?
4. What animals do mountain lions eat?
5. At what times of the day are mountain lions most active?

INDEX

ABOUT THE AUTHOR

Kim Thompson has been an animal lover ever since she was little. She loves to watch animals and photograph them, especially in the wild. She thinks that learning about animals can inspire people to take actions that help animals survive on the planet we share.